TRANSITIONING INTO JUNIOR HIGH SCHOOL

YOUR PASSPORT TO SUCCESS IN JUNIOR HIGH SCHOOL

C.D. Minnis B.Sc., M.Ed.

Copyright © 2017 Carol D. Minnis

All rights reserved. In accordance with U.S. Copyright Act of 1976, the scanning, uploading and electronic sharing of any part of this book without permission of the publisher constitute unlawful piracy and theft of the author's intellectual property. No part of this book may be reproduced in any form by any electronic or mechanical means (including photocopying, recording or information storage and retrieval) without permission in writing from the author or publisher. Thank you for your support of the author's rights.

Published by Richter Publishing LLC www.richterpublishing.com

ISBN: 1945812079

ISBN-13: 9781945812071

DISCLAIMER

This book is designed to provide information on education only. This information is provided and sold with the knowledge that the publisher and author do not offer any legal or medical advice. In the case of a need for any such expertise, consult with the appropriate professional. This book does not contain all information available on the subject. This book has not been created to be specific to any individual people or organization's situation or needs. Reasonable efforts have been made to make this book as accurate as possible. However, there may be typographical and/or content errors. Therefore, this book should serve only as a general guide. This book contains information that might be dated or erroneous and is intended only to educate and entertain. The author and publisher shall have no liability or responsibility to any person or entity regarding any loss or damage incurred, or alleged to have incurred, directly or indirectly, by the information contained in this book or as a result of anyone acting or failing to act upon the information in this book. You hereby agree never to sue and to hold the author and publisher harmless from any and all claims arising out of the information contained in this book. You hereby agree to be bound by this disclaimer, covenant not to sue and release. You may return this book within the guaranteed time period for a full refund. In the interest of full disclosure, this book contains affiliate links that might pay the author or publisher a commission upon any purchase from the company. While the author and publisher take no responsibility for any virus or technical issues that could be caused by such links, the business practices of these companies and/or the performance of any product or service, the author or publisher has used the product or service and makes a recommendation in good faith based on that experience. All characters appearing in this work have given permission for their photos to be published. Any resemblance to real persons, living or dead, is purely coincidental. The opinions and stories in this book are the views of the author and not that of the publisher.

DEDICATED TO OUR MOTHER
EVELYN GERTRUDE TAYLOR-MINNIS
NOVEMBER 15TH, 1935- NOVEMBER 20TH, 2016

You were the best woman any child could have had for a mother. We were blessed to be raised by you. Your selflessness was remarkable. Not only did you make us, your children, feel loved, but you had a gift of making each person you came into contact with feel special. To know you, was to love you.

Thank you for teaching us how to be respectful, honest, obedient, generous and resilient. More importantly, thank you for teaching us to fear God and walk in His ways.

ACKNOWLEDGEMENTS

Editors: Mrs. Suzanne Knowles - Ministry of Education
Mrs. Dellie Robinson -Thompson, Language Arts Teacher, Government High School
Ms. Joan Norman - former Language Arts Department Head at St. Anne's School
Mrs. Barbara Petersen – Professional Proofreading Services, New Jersey, USA

Mrs. Nixon - Former Principal of L.W. Young Junior High School
Mrs. Tiffany Barr - Former Guidance Counselor at L.W. Young Junior High School
Mrs. Shantell Smith - Guidance Counselor at S.C. McPherson Junior High School

Artists: Antonia Deveaux - C.V. Bethel Senior High School
Timothy Kabiga - St. Anne's High School
Leroy Nottage - Doris Johnson Senior High School

Kateleen Wells - Queen's College
Anita Williams - St. Augustine College
Sade Holness - S.C. McPherson Junior High School
Joel Johnson - L.W. Young Junior High School
Antoine Charles - L.W. Young Junior High School
Styr Marinard - St. Augustine's College
Keano Tonny - St. John's College
Ari & Hosea Hinsey - Andros
Alexander Carey - S.C. McPherson Junior High School
Royal Bahamas Defence Rangers: Rudy Stubbs - S.C. McPherson Junior High School
Sheldon Newton - S.C. McPherson Junior High School
Bernard Saunders - S.C. McPherson Junior High School
Omar Davis - D.W. Davis Junior High School

Urban Renewal Cadets: Jonniece Saunders
Donna Nottage
Lamika Nottage
Jade Saunders

INTRODUCTION

Students entering Junior High School undoubtedly do so with reservation and apprehension. Children feel fearful and anxious about going to a new school and a new environment. There will be new students and new teachers they have to get to know. Students will take more subjects than they were taking in Primary School.

The objective of this book is to help the grade 7 student settle as quickly as possible, so he/she can be about the business of learning. Every school age child in Junior High School, in the Commonwealth of The Bahamas, from Inagua in the south to Grand Bahama in the north, can benefit from using this book.

In the absence of a Guidance Counselor, the student, with the help of the Homeroom teacher, Family Life teacher and parent can still use the materials in this book. The information required will place the counselor or teacher in a better position to assist the student.

From this book, the student will learn:
a. Ways to help him/her successfully survive Junior High school.
b. Study skills to perform better in school.
c. Anger management and conflict resolution skills.
d. How to properly use the internet.
e. Money management skills at an early age.

The grade 7 student will learn valuable skills that will benefit him/her for the rest of his/her life.

Additionally, parents are asked to play an active role in the life of their child by utilizing the tools included in this book. These tools will help active and involved parents monitor their child's progress.

I wish a smooth transition into Junior High School for every child and parent who uses this book.

C.D. Minnis

7 Reasons the Student Needs This Book:

1. You will **SETTLE** quickly into the rudiments of your new school.

2. You will **CULTIVATE** school spirit for your new school.

3. You will set **EXPECTATIONS** and **GOALS** for yourself, and you will **DETERMINE** how you will achieve them.

4. You will form a closer **BOND** with your parents.

5. You will **UNDERSTAND** and **APPRECIATE** the role of your Guidance Counselor /teacher.

6. You will **GET ALONG** with friends and classmates.

7. You will be a **SUPERSUCCESSFUL** student.

7 Reasons Parents Need This Book:

1. You will be able to monitor the **SUCCESS** of your child's academic performance.

2. You will **PARTNER** with the school to ensure the success of your child.

3. You will be more **AWARE** of challenges your child may be experiencing in school.

4. You will be more **INVOLVED** in the development of your child's physical, mental, spiritual and social life.

5. You will **UNDERSTAND** that your child needs you, as a parent, to be actively involved in his/her life.

6. You will form a **CLOSER BOND** with your child.

7. You will **APPRECIATE** the important role the Guidance Counselor/teacher plays in the life of your child.

7 Reasons the Guidance Counselor/ Teacher Needs This Book:

1. You will be more **SUCCESSFUL** with your students.

2. You will have more **CONTACT** with your students' parents.

3. You will work **CLOSER** with administrators and teachers.

4. You will **FEEL BETTER** about your role in the life of the students.

5. You will be better **ORGANIZED**.

6. You will feel **LESS STRESSED**.

7. You will be more **RESPECTED** as a professional.

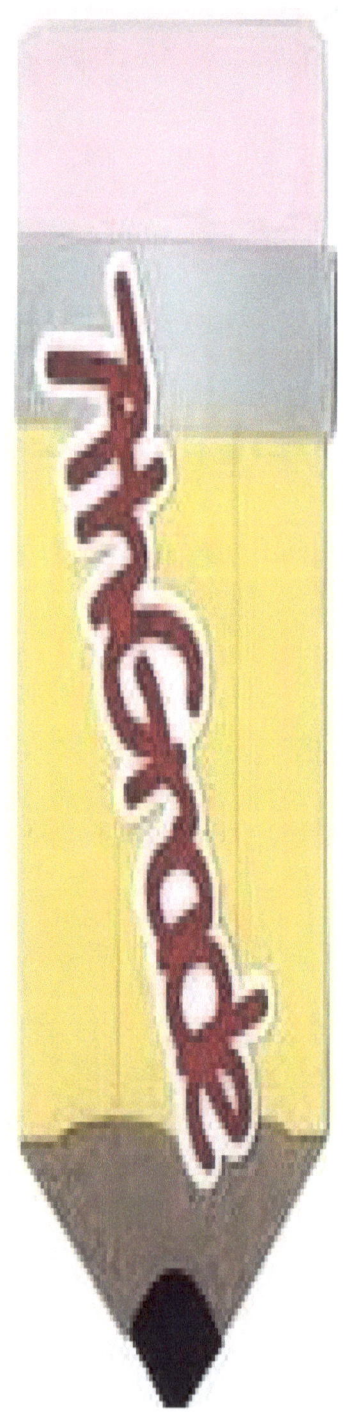

JUNIOR HIGH SCHOOL
Table of Contents

Chapter 1……The Journey Begins ……………………… 11

Chapter 2 ….. Results Oriented ……………………….. 16

Chapter 3……Your Guidance Counselor ……..……... 21

Chapter 4……Study Skills…………………..….……. 25

Chapter 5……I am Special…………………………… 30

Chapter 6 ….. Proper Use of the Internet &

Electronic Devices…………….... …….. 37

Chapter 7……Anger Management………………..….. 41

Chapter 8……Conflict Resolution…………….….….. 48

Chapter 9……Smart Saver……………………….…... 53

Chapter 10…. Parental Involvement……………..…... 58

Appendix A…Student Progress Report ………………..64
Appendix B.. Emergency Contact Numbers …………. .65
Appendix C…School Supplies……………………....….66
Appendix D… Student Information Sheet …………….67
Appendix E… Group Counseling Consent Form ……..69
Appendix F… Individual Counseling Consent Form…71
Appendix G … Certificate of Completion ……..……..73

Chapter 1
The Journey Begins - Grade 7

Letter to Parent/Guardian

Dear Parent/Guardian,

We are starting chapter 1 on _____ (Date). In this chapter, your child will learn new and exciting information about his/her new school. A police officer will be invited to speak about rules and laws. Additionally, the school's Senior Master or Mistress will make a presentation to the students on the importance of obeying the school's rules.

By the end of this section, your child will learn the importance of keeping order in the classroom, the school, the community and in the country. Also, he/she will know the school's patron and the administrative team.

Warmest regards,

_____
Guidance Counselor/Teacher

BONDING ACTIVITY
Name three former principals of your school. If necessary, take your child to the public library to research this information.
1. _____
2. _____
3. _____

Peter 5:7 - "Cast all your anxiety upon him for he cares for you."
2 Timothy 1:7 - "God did not give us the spirit of fear, but a spirit of power and of love and of self-discipline."

Description of my new school

The name of my Junior High School is _____

Address of my school: _____

Telephone number(s): _____

Which year did your school open?_____

Who is your school named after? _____

What was his/her profession? _____

List at least three persons who served as principal of your school:

1. _____
2. _____
3. _____

THE ADMINISTRATIVE TEAM - The Principal heads the school. Your school may have two Vice-Principals, two Senior Masters and two Senior Mistresses.

1. My new Principal's name is _____
2. The Vice-Principals' names are_____
   and _____
3. The Senior Masters' names are _____
   and _____
4. The Senior Mistresses' names are _____
   and _____

HOMEROOM TEACHER - You may have one or two homeroom teachers who will mark you present each day when you are at school and absent when you are not at school. Your homeroom teacher(s) may be one of your subject teachers, as well.

My homeroom teachers' names are _____ and

_____

My homeroom is _____ (e.g., 7S), and we are in room _____

There are _____ students in my homeroom class.

My school house (team) is _____

My house (team) color is _____

My School's Vision Statement: _____

_____

My School's Mission Statement: _____

_____
_____

The School's Prayer: _____

_____
_____
_____

The School's Pledge: _____

_____

The School's Motto: _____

The Words of the School's Song:

_____
_____
_____
_____
_____
_____
_____
_____
_____
_____
_____
_____
_____
_____
_____
_____

Paste a picture of the School's Mascot in the box

> **Instruction:** Students will create a poster, jingle, poem or rap that contains the school's rules.

SCHOOL NURSE - The nurse is assigned to your school in case you have a medical emergency during the day. The nurse can refer you for further help from a doctor or hospital.

The name of my school's nurse is

1. _____

SECURITY OFFICER(S) – The security officer(s) are stationed at the entrance of your school to check all visitors coming on campus to ensure they do not harm you. Periodically, the security officer(s) will patrol the campus to make sure you are safe.

The names of my school's security officers are

1. _____
2. _____

The support staff will help maintain a clean, green, and pristine environment for you to learn and grow in. Name your school's support staff. Our janitors are

1. _____
2. _____
3. _____
4. _____

The yardman is _____

SUCCESSFUL FIRST DAYS OF SCHOOL → **EXCELLENT YEAR WITH EXCELLENT RESULTS**

I acknowledge my child has successfully completed chapter 1.

_____   _____
Parent/Guardian's Signature   Date

CHAPTER 2
Results Oriented

Letter to Parent/Guardian

Dear Parent/Guardian,
We are starting chapter 2 on _____(Date).
In chapter 2, your child will learn about the importance of wearing proper uniform to school each day. Additionally, we will look at your child's daily timetable. He/she will also learn about The Bahamas Junior Certificate examinations that he/she will take while attending this Junior High School.

Warmest regards,

_____
Guidance Counselor/Teacher

BONDING ACTIVITY
Study the school's dress code with your child so that he/she will always be properly attired. Together with your child, list five (5) uniformed professions.

1. _____
2. _____
3. _____
4. _____
5. _____

Jeremiah 29:11 – "For I know the plans I have for you, declares the LORD, plans to prosper you and not to harm you, plans to give you hope and a future."

> Am I in the right school?
> Will I like my teachers?
> Will I make new friends?
> How will I be graded?
> Will I get along with my classmates?

The Pre-Socratic Greek philosopher, Heraclitus says, "The only thing constant is change." You have started Junior High School, and your Primary School days are behind you. How do you cope with these changes? Do you join a club or organization? Do you take new and challenging classes? Do you socialize with new friends?

Give two ways how you will cope with being in Junior High School.

1. _____
2. _____

Junior High School uniform maybe different from Primary School. Describe your school's uniform

Socks _____

Shoes _____

Skirt _____

Pants _____

Crest _____

Criss-cross tie _____

Necktie _____

Blouse _____

Shirt _____

Paste a picture of you in your new school uniform.

EXERCISE AND TEXTBOOKS - You will need to have a different exercise book for each class. You will get more subjects in Junior High School than you got while at the Primary School level. You will have a different teacher for each subject.

	STUDENT'S TIMETABLE				
	MONDAY	**TUESDAY**	**WEDNESDAY**	**THURSDAY**	**FRIDAY**
PERIOD 1 SUBJECT TEACHER ROOM					
PERIOD 2 SUBJECT TEACHER ROOM					
PERIOD 3 SUBJECT TEACHER ROOM					
PERIOD 4 SUBJECT TEACHER ROOM					
PERIOD 5 SUBJECT TEACHER ROOM					

My first year at _____ will be _____
(Name of school)
(Happy, productive, meaningful, positive, etc. or use your own descriptive to fill in the blank)

Instruction: To promote school spirit, each student will create a 4-minute Photo Story about his/her new school entitled, *"My school is the best school in The Bahamas."*

TESTS AND QUIZZES - Your teachers will test you periodically to ascertain your understanding of the lessons covered. The Bahamas Junior Certificate (**BJC**) is administered in grade 9. Students in the public schools will need a minimum of four (4) B.J.C.'s as one of the requirements to graduate from Senior High School and receive the Bahamas High School Diploma. Subjects offered are:

Art	Craft	General Science	Mathematics
Language Arts	Home Economics	Health Science	Technical Drawing
Religious Studies	Social Studies	English Literature	

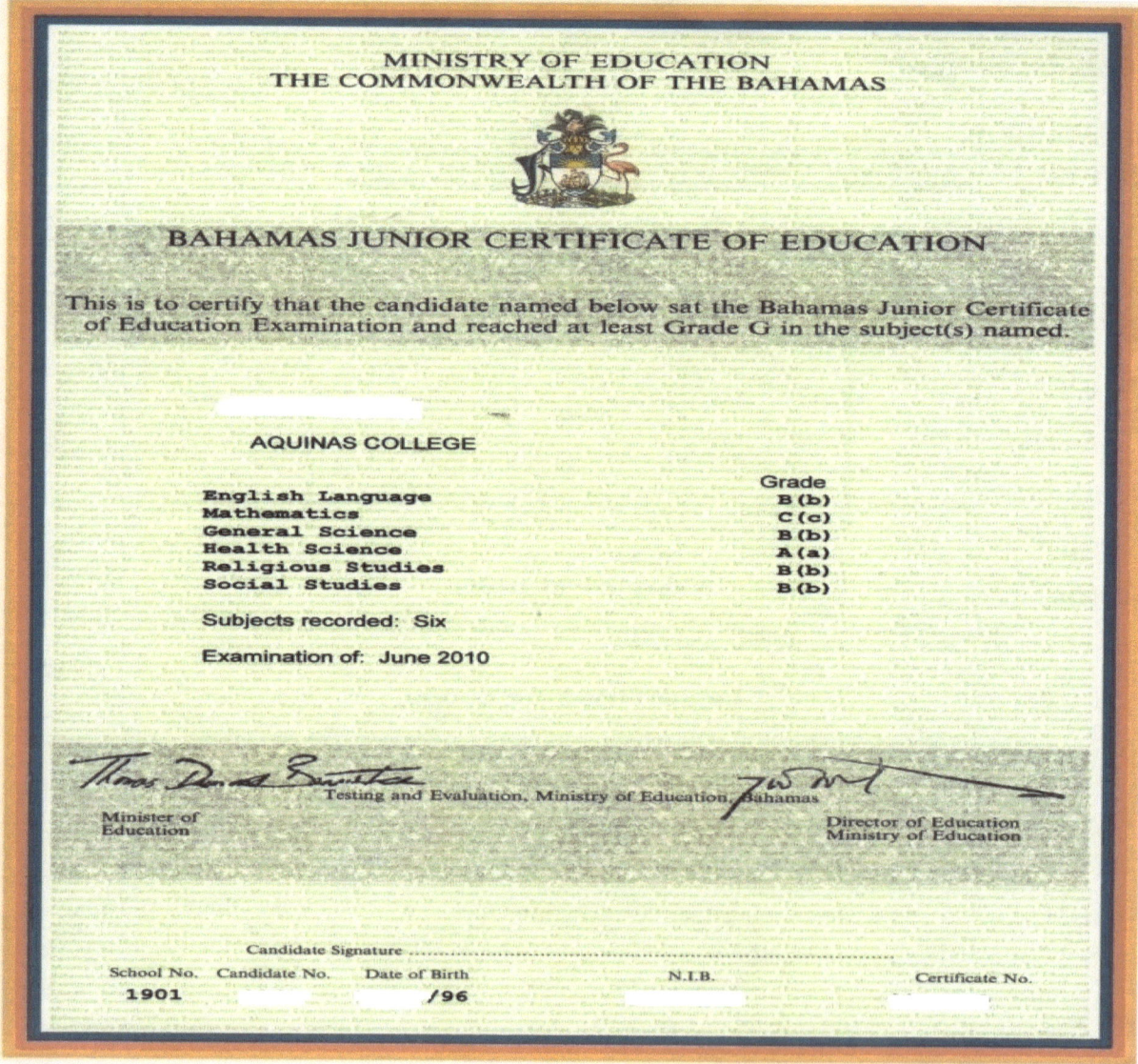

I acknowledge my child has successfully completed chapter 2.

_____   _____

Parent/Guardian's Signature   Date

CHAPTER 3
YOUR GUIDANCE COUNSELOR

Letter to Parent/Guardian

Dear Parent/Guardian,
We are starting chapter 3 on _____ (Date). In chapter 3, we will learn about the important role of the Guidance Counselor in the school. Your child will understand and appreciate that he/she can always seek the assistance of the counselor for personal/social issues, academic help and career planning.

Warmest regards,

_____
Guidance Counselor/Teacher

BONDING ACTIVITY

Assist your child by listing some ways he/she can receive assistance from the Guidance Counselor.

1. _____
   _____
2. _____
   _____
3. _____
   _____
4. _____
   _____

Proverbs 1:5 – "Let the wise hear and increase in learning and the one who understands obtain guidance."

Your school may have more than one Guidance Counselor. Your Guidance Counselor will work along with the administrative team, the teachers and your parents to ensure you have a meaningful Junior High School experience.

WHEN DO YOU NEED TO SEE YOUR COUNSELOR?
- Are you anxious about your new school and finding it difficult to adjust?
- Do you feel overwhelmed by being in a bigger school with more students?
- Do you feel there are too many subjects for you to learn?

These are all good reasons to visit your Guidance Counselor.

Talk To Your Counselor. Sometimes it is hard to trust other people. Your school counselor will help you overcome shyness, resist peer pressure and deal with stress. You are not alone. You can trust your counselor who will be there for you.

What's On Your Mind?
Are you having trouble in school?
Are you getting along with other students?
Are you being bullied?
Are you worried about something that is happening at home?
Think about what you want to talk about so you can tell your counselor everything and get help.

Listen To Your Counselor. Depending on the reason you are visiting your counselor, you may get possible solutions to a problem. You and your counselor will brainstorm together and figure out several ideas for solving your problem. Your counselor may have to call your parents or refer you to an outside agency to help with your problem. The solution will only work if you listen to your counselor and then make a commitment to follow through with necessary changes.

Be Open and Honest. Benjamin Franklin said, "Honesty is the Best Policy." Always tell the truth even when it may get you in trouble. However, being open is a little different from being honest. When you are open, it means you are saying what is on your mind. So, you must be open and honest if you want your counselor to help you.

COUNSELORS CAN HELP IN TOUGH TIMES: Talk to your counselor if you have academic challenges, problems with others, alcohol or other drug abuse, sexuality challenges or depression. Your counselor will also assist you with deciding upon your future career.

You are always welcomed in the counselor's office. So make an appointment or just drop in to see your counselor today.

I acknowledge my child has successfully completed chapter 3.

_____   _____
Parent/Guardian's Signature   Date

CHAPTER 4
STUDY SKILLS

Letter to Parent/Guardian

Dear Parent/Guardian,
We are starting chapter 4 on _____ (Date).
In this section, your child will learn how to develop sound study habits. He/she will also learn tips on how to study for examinations.

Warmest regards,

_____
Guidance Counselor/Teacher

BONDING ACTIVITY

Sit with your child and create a workable study timetable your child will be able to follow each day.

Day	Time	Time	Time	Time
Monday				
Tuesday				
Wednesday				
Thursday				
Friday				
Saturday				
Sunday				

Proverbs 10:17 – "Whoever heeds instruction is on the path to life, but he who rejects reproof leads others astray."

It is important for you to know your learning style. Knowing your learning style will help you formulate the appropriate approach to studying.

KNOW YOUR LEARNING STYLE

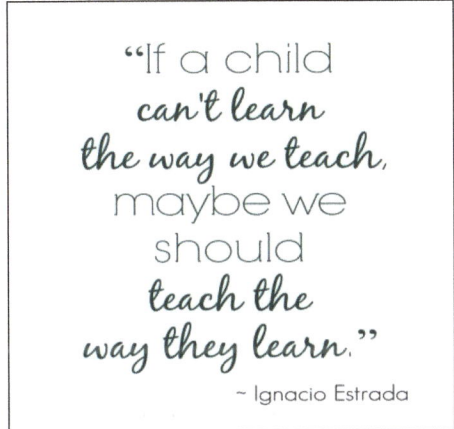

PRACTICE GOOD STUDY HABITS

1. Clear off a desk or table and stack your books to one side so that you can reach them quickly.
2. Get into your work quickly. Do not take phone calls or have visitors during your study period.
3. Have a pen, pencil and enough paper on hand for use when needed.
4. Do homework first if any. Next review all school work for that day.
5. Follow study schedule.
6. If you don't have a room of your own where you can shut noises out, ask your family to make an effort to be quiet during your study periods.
7. Write potential test questions and answer them without looking at your notes.
8. When you are through studying, let a friend or family member test you.
9. Study for one (1) hour. Take a 10-minute break. Study for another one (1) hour. Study for at least two (2) hours each night.
10. Study your hardest subjects first (when your mind is fresh).
11. Review what you studied after you are finished. Do this by closing the book and summing up the facts and ideas in your words.
12. Reward yourself after you have finished studying. Watch a special T.V. program or enjoy Facebook time. Enjoy your reward for a job well done.

Courtesy of "How To Get Good Grades."

"To succeed, we must first Believe we can." Michael Korda

The Following Will Cause Poor Concentration:

Noise	Hunger/Poor diet	T.V./Music
Lack of sleep	Worry	Poor attention span
Boredom	Dislike of subject	Lack of interest
Daydreaming	Phone/iPad/Computer	Constant interruptions

Your teachers will give you many tests. They will test to see how well you understood the objectives of the lesson and to measure your ability to cope with the material taught.

HOW TO ACE YOUR TESTS

1. **SKIM THE TEST QUICKLY.** Knowing what is on the exam will help you budget your time wisely.
2. **READ THE DIRECTIONS CAREFULLY.** If you are not clear about something in the instructions, ask.
3. **DON'T BE AFRAID TO SKIP A QUESTION.** Answer questions you are confident of first. Come back, if you have time, to respond to the questions you did not answer.
4. **LOOK FOR "CLUE WORDS."** On a multiple choice or true/false test, words such as, always, none, all and everybody usually means you can eliminate that choice.
5. **CHECK YOUR WORK.** Ensure you have crossed your T's and dotted your I's. Careless mistakes lead to wrong answers.

What to do before a test:
Match the correct answer on the right with the stem on the left.

STEM	ANSWER
1._____ Make a "Study Sheet"	A. Review for the test with one or more friends.
2._____ Dress for success	B. Studying the night before the exam for the first time
3._____ Make flash cards	C. Create your test by thinking of questions the teacher may ask you on the examination.
4._____ Eat breakfast	D. Write key facts about each subject, e.g., Formulas in Math or Science, dates in History.
5._____ Create a Practice Test	E. Eat the morning of the test.
6._____ Study with a buddy	F. Wear comfortable clothes on test day.
7._____ Take the supplies you need	G. Write points to review everything from vocabulary words to Math facts.
8._____ Do not cram	H. Set out everything you will need the night before.

Courtesy of "The Parent Institute."

Photo courtesy of www.fodors.com

Mount Alvernia, Cat Island, Bahamas
"Aim high. Be the best you can be." C.D. Minnis

Study! Study! Study some more. You will have to study every night. However, you should do assigned homework first. You must read over all the work you did that day, and read ahead for the upcoming lessons. Then follow your study timetable. As you prepare to create your study timetable, look at all the activities you have each day.

E.g., Tuesdays – 3:15 p.m. – 5:15 p.m.: Debate practice
Thursdays – 3:15 p.m. – 4:15 p.m.: Band practice
Saturdays – 9:00 a.m. – 11:00 a.m.: Track practice

STUDY TIMETABLE

TIME	4p.m.-5a.m.	5p.m.-6p.m.	6p.m.-7p.m.	7p.m.-8p.m.	8p.m.-9p.m.	9p.m.-10p.m.	
MONDAY		MATHS		PE			
TUESDAY					SS		
WEDNESDAY		ENGLISH		GENERAL SCIENCE			
THURSDAY				CIVICS			
FRIDAY							
TIME	9a.m.-10a.m.	10a.m.-11a.m.	11a.m.-12a.m.	12p.m.-1p.m.	1p.m.-2p.m.	2p.m.-3p.m.	3p.m.-4p.m.
SATURDAY					CRAFT		
SUNDAY							
TIME	4p.m.-5p.m.	5p.m.-6p.m.	6p.m.-7p.m.	7p.m.-8p.m.	8p.m.-9p.m.	9p.m.-10p.m.	
SATURDAY							
SUNDAY		MUSIC					

Answer key for *"How To Ace Your Test:"* 1. D, 2. F, 3. G, 4. E, 5. C, 6. A, 7. H, 8. B

I acknowledge my child has successfully completed chapter 4.

_____   _____

Parent/Guardian's Signature   Date

CHAPTER 5
I AM SPECIAL

Letter to Parent/Guardian

Dear Parent/Guardian,
We are starting chapter 5 on _____(Date). Your child will appreciate and value himself/herself as an individual who is uniquely and wonderfully created by God. He/she will understand that his/her gifts and talents should determine his/her future career.

Warmest regards,

_____
Guidance Counselor/Teacher

BONDING ACTIVITY

Help your child write a list of positive descriptors about himself/herself.

Assist your child with mapping your family tree.

_____
_____
_____
_____
_____
_____

Proverbs 3:5-6 "Trust in the LORD with all your heart and lean not on your understanding; in all your ways acknowledge Him, and He will direct your path."

"Making a difference is not an accident or
unexpected occurrence of the times.
People choose to make a difference." Maya Angelou

MY FAMILY TREE

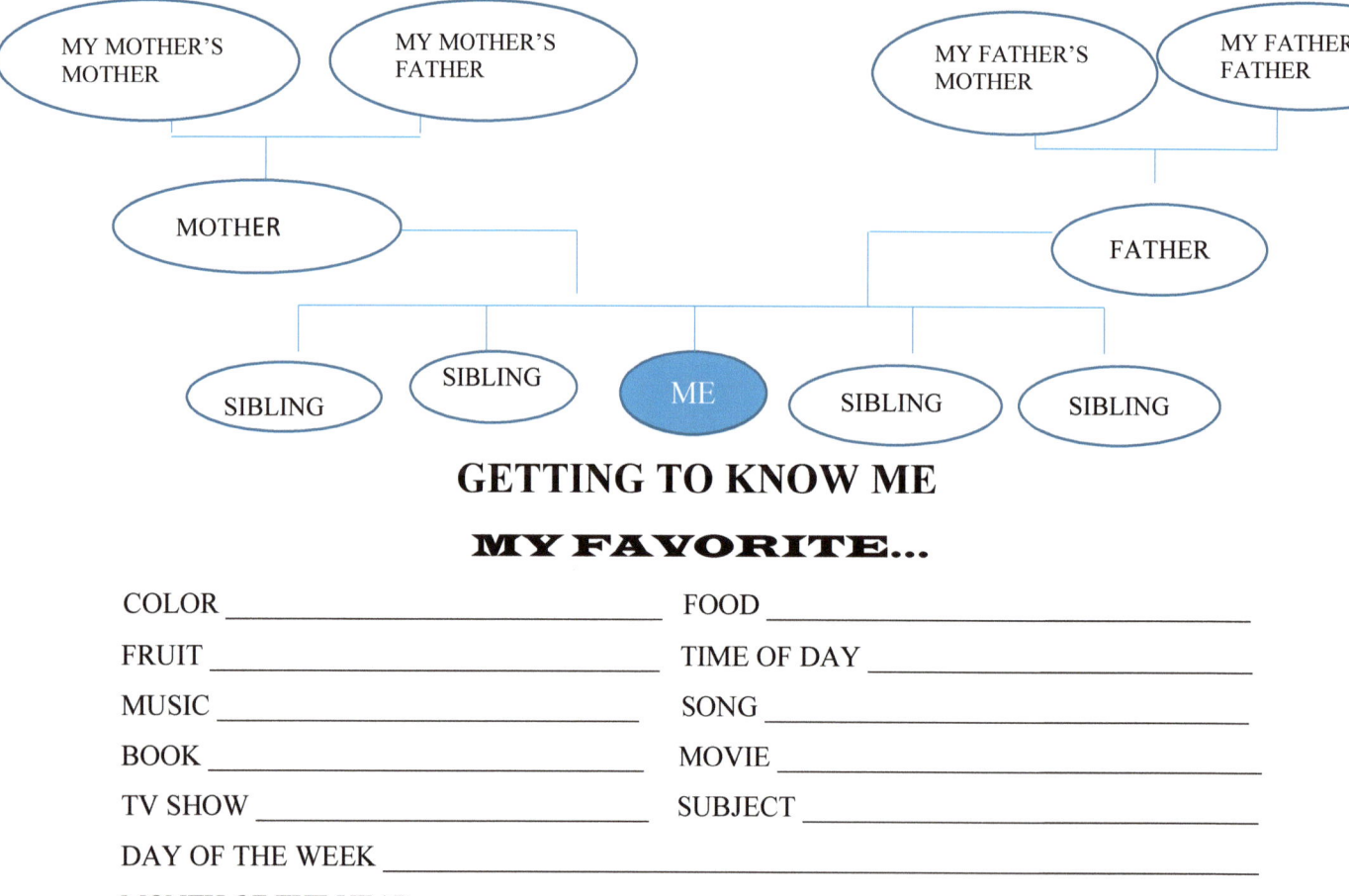

GETTING TO KNOW ME

MY FAVORITE...

COLOR _____ FOOD _____

FRUIT _____ TIME OF DAY _____

MUSIC _____ SONG _____

BOOK _____ MOVIE _____

TV SHOW _____ SUBJECT _____

DAY OF THE WEEK _____

MONTH OF THE YEAR _____

"YOU BECOME A LEADER WHEN YOU DECIDE NOT TO BE A COPY BUT AN ORIGINAL." DR. MYLES MUNROE

Instructions: Students will:
  A. Interview parents, grandparents, godparents, cousins, neighbors, to collect data from his/her life. He/she will then create a timeline of himself/herself from birth to present.   OR
  B. Draw a picture of him/her doing his/her favorite activity (e.g. playing a basketball game, video games, baking, etc.)   OR
  C. Create a collage of himself/herself using pictures from baby to present.

NBA Superstar is what I want to be

EXPLORING YOUR CAREER INTEREST

It is crucial for you to identify your passion early in Junior High School. What do you enjoy doing most? Read the following statements and circle which ones apply to you.

My classes will prepare me for my future career.	YES	NO
I will go to college after high school.	YES	NO
I will go to vocational/technical or trade school after high school.	YES	NO
I will start working after high school.	YES	NO
I love working with animals.	YES	NO
I love working with plants.	YES	NO
I love working with electronics.	YES	NO
I want to work in an office.	YES	NO
I love working with children.	YES	NO
I want to work with computers.	YES	NO
I want to work with the geriatrics (old people).	YES	NO
I want to be a professional athlete.	YES	NO

Confucius says, "If you love what you do, you will never work a day in your life." You should take classes that would prepare you for your future.

SUBJECTS	CAREER POSSIBILITIES
Agriculture	Soil Chemist, Nursery operator, Farmer, Teacher, Landscaper
Building Trades	Carpenter, Contractor, Cabinet Maker, Architect, Building Inspector, Teacher
Commercial Arts	Teacher, Sculptor, Graphic or Advertising Designer, Calligrapher, Ceramist
Family & Consumer Science	Interior designer, Food & Beverage Manager, Chef, Dietician, Teacher
Performing Arts	Music Specialist, Teacher, Musicologist, Composer/lyrics, Disc Jokey

The Guidance Department will organize a career fair and professionals from different industries will be invited to present the details of their jobs to the students. Students may be given the opportunity to dress as the professional they wish to become in the future.

The student will sign a contract outlining short-term goals and long-term goals he/she will accomplish.

My Personal Contract

I, _____ (student's name) agree I will name my goals, set dates for accomplishing my goals and work hard to achieve each short-term goal and each long-term goal.

SHORT-TERM GOALS	
Goals	**Date of Accomplishment**
1.	
2.	
3.	
4.	
5.	
Others:	

LONG-TERM GOALS	
Goals	**Date of Accomplishment**
1.	
2.	
3.	
4.	
5.	
Others:	

Please print name: _____

Student's signature: _____

Date: _____

LIVING THE BAHAMIAN DREAM

It is always important to dream. But, as you dream and plan your future, always remember to be faithful to God, country, family and yourself.

Your school, the first computer, the first airplane, the first mall were all built because someone had a dream. What do you dream about achieving in life? Create your "Bahamian Dream."

Instructions:
1. Make a list of all the things you want in life (good grades, career, tablet, clothes, car, home, vacations, etc.)
2. Collect pictures of these items (magazines, computer)
3. Get a large poster board (Choose your favorite color)
4. Paste the photos on the board
5. Mount your dream board where you can see it every day to keep you motivated

AFFIRM YOURSELF EVERY DAY

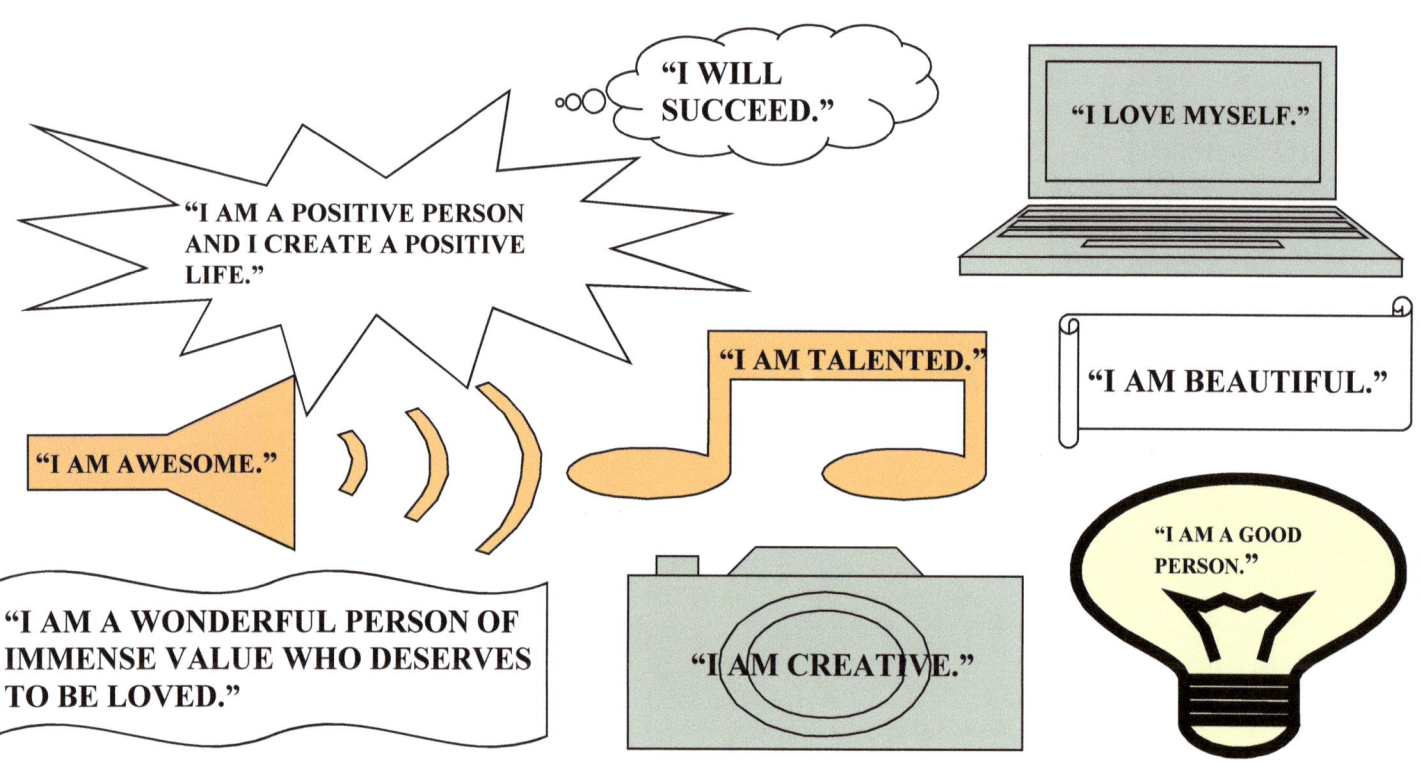

Write some positive attributes about yourself.

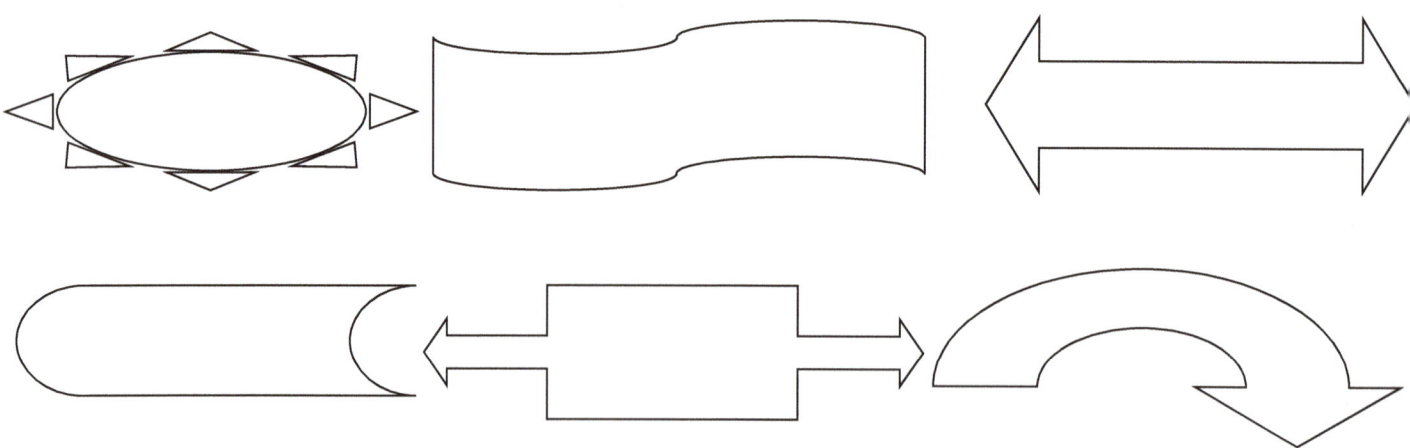

I acknowledge my child has successfully completed chapter 5.

_____   _____
Parent/Guardian's Signature   Date

CHAPTER 6
PROPER USE OF THE INTERNET & ELECTRONIC DEVICES

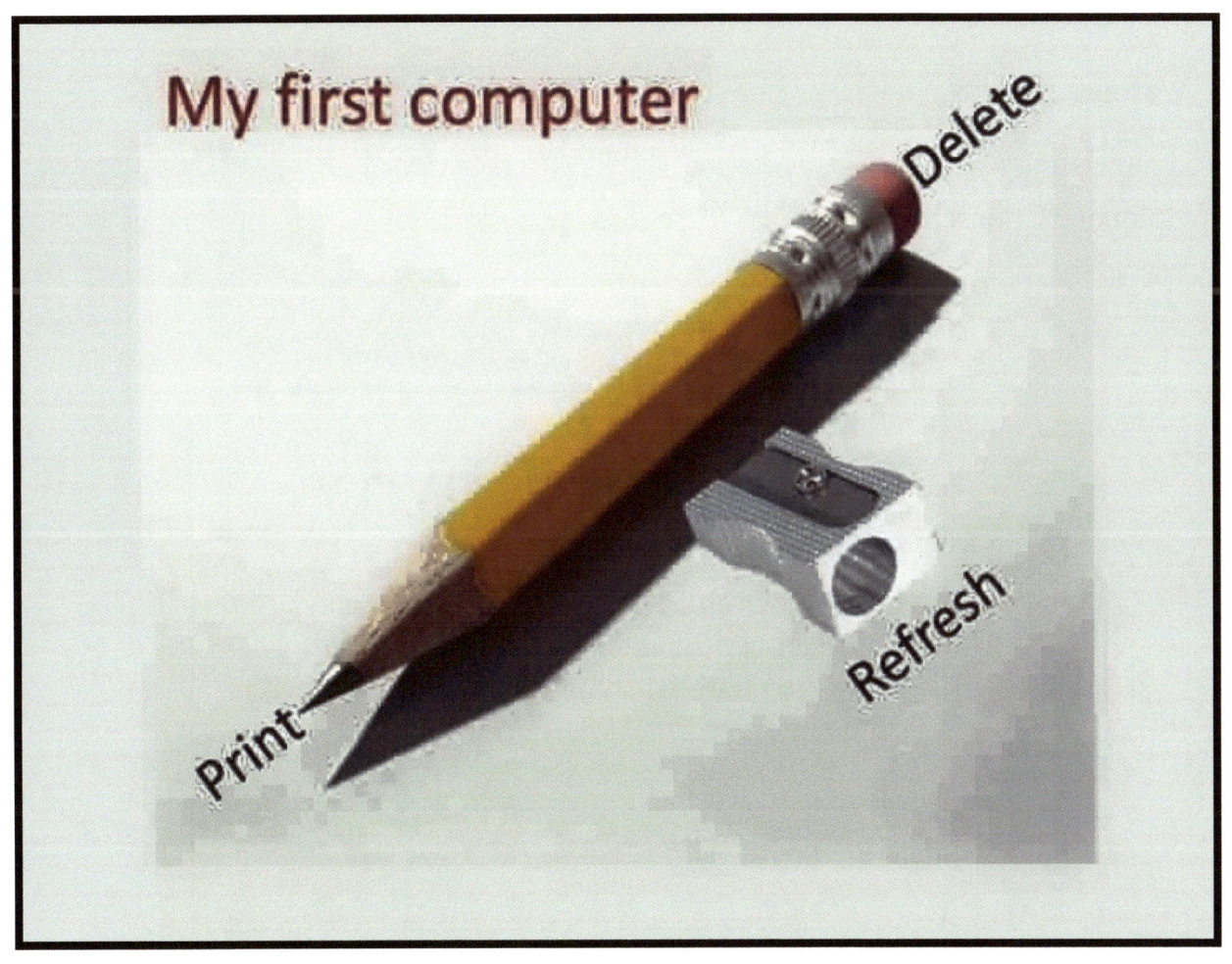

Letter to Parent/Guardian

Dear Parent/Guardian,
We are starting chapter 6 on _____(Date).
In this chapter, your child will learn about the benefits of responsibly using the internet. A guest speaker will be invited to address students on the topic, *"The computer can make a positive difference or have a devastating impact on your life."*

Warmest regards,

_____
Guidance Counselor/Teacher

BONDING ACTIVITY

Sit with your child and list some of the ways he/she can use the internet to do schoolwork. Have your child list some ways he/she will never use the internet.

_____
_____
_____
_____
_____
_____

Ephesians 5:15 – "Look carefully then how you walk, not as unwise but as wise."

According to Annunciation BVM Catholic Elementary on *Internet Safety*, "The internet is an incredible tool that can benefit a student in many positive ways if used correctly."
- You can research schoolwork to receive excellent grades.
- You can type and save your work on the computer, spell-check and grammar check.
- You can copy and paste pictures off the internet into your schoolwork to enhance the overall appearance of your work.
- Downloading educational apps to help with homework and classwork is a fantastic option too.

**Directions: Place students in groups of five (5). A fun and easy way to separate students into groups are to use Skittles, M & M's or colored rubber bands. Students will be grouped based on the color they selected. Each team will choose one form of technology and show how their chosen technology can be utilized in the classroom.
(Examples of technology to choose from: iPhone, iPod, Game devices, Kindle, Tablet, Smartphone, MP3 player, Computer, etc.)**

You are on the World Wide Web if you have:
- ever posted a comment or reply on the internet,
- uploaded a video to YouTube,
- posted a picture on Facebook, Twitter or any other social network.

Remember the world has access to the web. More than 4.5 billion people using the internet will have access to your information. Children find the internet easy to use and like to use it for fun, games, email, chat and instant messaging. The internet is accessible through the computer, cell phones or iPads/tablets.

When using the internet, ask yourself the following questions:
1. Would I embarrass or hurt anyone by what I have posted?
2. How would my parents and teachers feel about what I posted?
3. Can legal actions be taken against me because of what I posted?
4. Can what I posted stop me from getting a job later in life?
5. How would I feel if what I posted was published in the media?
6. Do I have a clear conscience about what I posted?

Instruction: Create a poster, poem or jingle depicting the proper or improper use of the internet.

You can use the internet to learn about our nation's leaders.

> **Instructions:** Place students in groups of 4 or 5. A fun and easy way to separate students into groups are to use Skittles, M & M's or colored rubber bands. Students will be grouped based on the color selected. Each team will choose one of the former Prime Ministers or the present Prime Minister and do in-depth research on the chosen person. The group will then present their research to the class in the form of a photo story, poem, rap, artwork, or a documentary story.

Unfortunately, many teenagers use the internet for negative reasons. If you post inappropriate pictures of yourself on the web via Youtube, Twitter, Facebook, WhatsApp or any other social network, the police can arrest and prosecute you.

One of the negative ways teenagers use the internet is to cyberbully. Some signs of cyberbullying to watch for are:

1. Avoiding friends and family members.
2. Slipping grades.
3. "Acting out" in anger at home.
4. Changes in mood, behavior, sleep, or appetite.
5. Wanting to stop using the computer or cell phone.
6. Appearing nervous or jumpy when getting an instant message or email.
7. Avoiding discussions about computer or mobile activities.

Courtesy of *"Cyberbullying & Sexting: What Parents Need to Know."*

When possible, you should block the bully from your online groups and profiles and on cell phones and email accounts. Do not respond. Keep the threatening messages, pictures and texts, as these are evidence for the bully's parents, school or even the police. If you are in the same class with the person who is cyberbullying you, tell your Guidance Counselor so something can be done right away to stop the bullying peacefully.

Adapted from "Cyberbullying: New problems, new tactics." www.kidshealth.org

I acknowledge my child has successfully completed chapter 6.

_____   _____
Parent/Guardian's Signature   Date

CHAPTER 7
ANGER MANAGEMENT

Letter to Parent/Guardian

Dear Parent/Guardian,

We are starting chapter 7 on _____ (Date). A juvenile parole officer will be invited to speak on *"Anger Management."* The officer will address teen violence and how making poor decisions can change one's future forever. By the end of this chapter, your child will learn skills to cope with anger.

Warmest regards,

_____
Guidance Counselor/Teacher

BONDING ACTIVITY

Sit with your child and have him/her create a list of five ways he/she can control his/her anger.

_____
_____
_____
_____
_____
_____

Ephesians 4:26 - "Be angry and do not sin..."

Anger is defined as an emotion, a feeling, a response to a perceived threat of pain – present, past or future. It can be real or imagined. Anger is associated with bitterness, hurt, child abuse, bullying, domestic violence and intimidation to name a few. One reacts to violence by either fighting or running away from the situation.

Anger can be triggered by any of the following actions:
1. Rude people
2. Traffic jams
3. Prejudice
4. Unkindness
5. False accusations/gossip
6. Criticism

When you find yourself getting angry you should:
1. Cool down
2. Walk away
3. Relax
4. Ask for clarification on the situation
5. Look at alternatives
6. Take responsibility for your emotional state
7. Practice thinking positive thoughts
8. See things from the other person's point of view

Remember the two R's – Reaction and Response. You cannot control someone else's reaction or response. You can only control your reaction and your response to a situation.

Instruction: Students will create an informational brochure about anger management and its adverse effects.

Fort Montague, Nassau, Bahamas

> *"Guard your thoughts, they become words;*
> *Guard your words, they become actions;*
> *Guard your actions, they become habits;*
> *Guard your habits, they become character;*
> *Guard your character, for it becomes your destiny."*
>
> Modified quote from Margaret Thatcher,
> Former Prime Minister of Great Britain

You must take ownership of your feelings and reactions to situations.

IT IS INACCURATE TO SAY….	SAY…
1. Patrick made me mad!	I choose to be mad.
2. Dad makes me furious!	I decide to be upset.
3. My brother makes me miserable!	I want to be miserable.
4. Mr. Brown's class makes me sick!	I choose to dislike Mr. Brown's class.
5. My mom makes me feel defeated!	I wish to feel defeated.
6. Barry made me feel ridiculous!	I prefer to feel silly.
7. My boyfriend/girlfriend frustrates me!	I decide to be frustrated.
8. The school makes me feel dumb!	I want to feel stupid.
9. My pastor makes me feel guilty!	I wish to feel guilty.
10. Traffic jams upset me!	I decide to be angry.

Courtesy of "Skills for Living."

"If we are ever to have real peace in this world we shall begin with the children." Gandhi

Self-assessment is a crucial tool in personal growth. Circle the word in each statement that describes your actions.

1	2	3	4	5
Never	Once in a while	Often	Most of the time	Always
I know when I am angry.			1 2 3 4 5	
I use techniques that assist me to gain control over my anger.			1 2 3 4 5	
I remember that I can walk away from situations.			1 2 3 4 5	
I am aware of my anger triggers.			1 2 3 4 5	
When I get angry, I remember the adverse impact losing my temper can cause.			1 2 3 4 5	
I feel I deal with my anger in constructive ways.			1 2 3 4 5	

CALMING EXERCISE

This self-calming exercise should help you relax and de-stress when you are at your boiling point:
1. Breathe out the anger, breathe in the calm.
2. Take slow, deep abdominal breaths.
3. Clench and unclench your fist.
4. Concentrate on calming things:
    a. Chatting on Facebook
    b. Your favorite computer game.
5. Reassure yourself, "This too will pass."
6. Let the anger go – It is not worth it.

"Holding on to anger is like grasping a hot coal with the intent of throwing it at someone else: You are the one who gets burned." Buddha

Anger Management

Across

4. Physical force exerted for the purpose of violating, damaging, or abusing
5. A feeling of intense dislike; enmity
7. The condition of feeling sad or despondent
9. Shrewd or devious management, especially for one's advantage.
10. Indignation or ill-will felt as a result of a real or imagined grievance.
11. A person who is habitually cruel or overbearing, especially to smaller or weaker people
12. Overbearing pride

Down

1. To hurt or injure by maltreatment; ill-use
2. Having or being a taste that is sharp, acrid, and unpleasant
3. To cause mental or emotional suffering to; distress
6. Compulsive physiological and psychological need for a habit-forming substance
8. To make timid; fill with fear

Answer to puzzle is on page 47

"Peace cannot be achieved through violence; it can only be attained through understanding." Ralph Walden Emerson

A LITTLE BOY'S TEMPER – GOD'S WORK

There once was a boy who had a terrible temper. His father gave him a bag of nails and told him every time he lost his temper he must hammer a nail into the back of the fence.

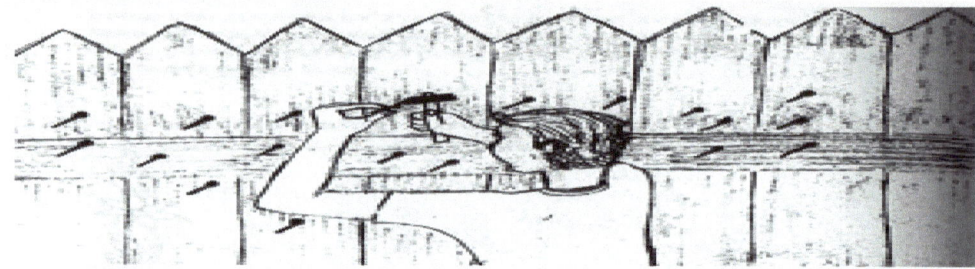

The first day the boy had driven 27 nails into the fence. Over the next few weeks, as he learned to control his anger, the number of nails hammered daily gradually dwindled down.

He discovered it was easier to hold his temper than to drive those nails into the fence. Finally, the day came when the boy didn't lose his temper.

He told his father about it. The father suggested the boy now pull out one nail for each day he was able to hold his temper.

Many days passed, and the young boy was finally able to tell his father all the nails were gone.

The father took his son by the hand and led him to the fence. He said, "You have done well, my son, but look at the holes in the fence. The fence will never be the same. When you say things in anger, they leave a scar just like this one. You can put a knife in a man and draw it out. It won't matter how many times you say I'm sorry; the wound is still there. A verbal wound is as bad as a physical one."

The boy looked up at his dad with tears in his eyes and said, "I understand now; thank you, dad." His father gave him a hug and said, "I know son; I love you." Both of them learned from this lesson and were forever changed by placing nails in the fence.   Remember…..

"ANGER" is just one letter short of "DANGER."

Author Unknown

Answers to Anger Management crossword puzzle

	1A		2B						3H		
	B		4V	I	O	L	E	N	C	E	U
	U			T						R	
	S			T				5H	6A	T	R	E	D
7D	E	P	R	E	S	S	I	O	N		D
				R					D		8I
		9M	A	N	I	P	U	L	A	T	I	O	N
				E					C		T
		10R	E	S	E	N	T	M	E	N	T
				S						I		M
										O		I
										N		D
												A
												T
								11B	U	L	L	Y	I	N	G
												O
						12A	R	R	O	G	A	N	C	E

I acknowledge my child has successfully completed chapter 7.

_____   _____

Parent/Guardian's Signature   Date

CHAPTER 8
CONFLICT RESOLUTION

Letter to Parent/Guardian

Dear Parent/Guardian,
We are starting chapter 8 on _____ (Date). In this section, your child will learn skills to resolve conflicts. A police officer will be invited to do a presentation on *"Conflict Resolution Skills."* By the end of this chapter, your child will be able to recognize situations which may cause conflict and will know how to avoid these situations.

Warmest regards,

_____
Guidance Counselor/Teacher

BONDING ACTIVITY

Together with your child, list the different types of conflict. Help your child identify positive ways he/she can resolve conflicts.

_____
_____
_____
_____
_____
_____
_____
_____
_____

Proverbs 15:1 – "A soft answer turns away wrath, but a harsh word stirs up anger."

In an arm wrestling contest, there is a winner and a loser. It is a friendly game to see who is physically stronger. Wouldn't it be a lot less complicated if we could handle all conflicts like we would an arm wrestling contest?

When we get angry, though, we see the other person as the enemy. The problem involves both individuals. It is not "me against you," but both characters locked together in a common situation that needs to be solved.

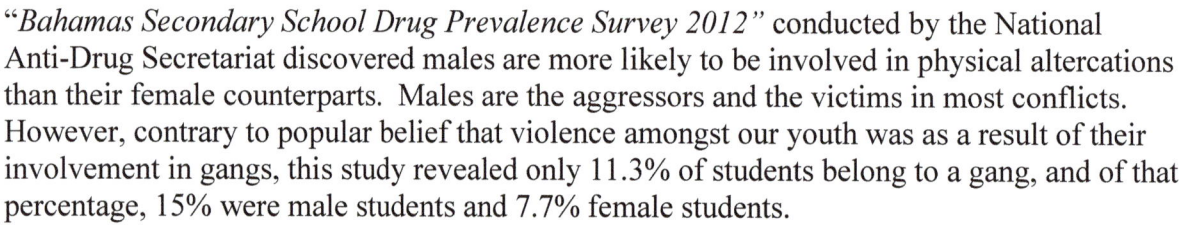

Remember …. Both parties should work towards resolving the conflict. You are both responsible for finding a peaceful solution to the conflict.

"Bahamas Secondary School Drug Prevalence Survey 2012" conducted by the National Anti-Drug Secretariat discovered males are more likely to be involved in physical altercations than their female counterparts. Males are the aggressors and the victims in most conflicts. However, contrary to popular belief that violence amongst our youth was as a result of their involvement in gangs, this study revealed only 11.3% of students belong to a gang, and of that percentage, 15% were male students and 7.7% female students.

Unscramble these sentences to discover some peaceful quotes, which could help you as you face conflicts:

1. "Ouy rtohw a lwbo, oyu og." - Carl Bethel, Former Minister of Education
   _____.

2. "Ew utms emocboe hte ahcneg ew tanw ot ese." Mahatma Gandhi
   _____.

3. "Eth imte si laayws igrth ot od hte igthr hgtri." Martin Luther King Jr.
   _____

4. "hte ecpea emkras lhlsa eb alcde eht ihlcrdne fo oGd." Matthew 5:9
   _____

5. "na eey ofr na yee asvlee deryybeov libnd." Martin Luther King Jr.
   _____

Answer to scrambled sentences on page 52

LOVE HAS OTHER NAMES SUCH AS...

FORGIVENESS	ENCOURAGE	SYMPATHY	AFFECTION
TOLERANCE	PATIENCE	EMPATHY	FRIENDLINESS
MERCY	HELP	PEACE	GOODWILL

NO MATTER HOW MUCH LOVE WE GIVE TO OTHERS,
… MORE RUSHES INTO TAKE ITS PLACE.
Multiple Authors

Read the following scenarios below. Write or draw an ending for each story.

"Girl Janet, Susan wrote on Facebook that you stole her smart phone."

"Yea, Susan said you are nothing but a thief. She said you stole $20 from her too."

How does Janet resolve this conflict?

"Terrance, free up the Oakley now!"

"Terrance, didn't you hear John said to free up the Oakley?"

How does Terrance resolve this conflict?

First Baptist Church, Nicholl's Town, North Andros, Bahamas
"Let us love one another, for God is love" 1 John 4:7

Instructions: Students will list the different types of conflicts. Students will role play various types of conflict, then give suggestions on the do's and don'ts as they critique each role play act.

Eco Summer Camp 2013 – Fresh Creek, Andros, Bahamas
"There is more fun playing than fighting." C.D. Minnis

Answers to scrambled sentences
1. "You throw a blow, you go." Carl Bethel, Former Minister of Education
2. "We must become the change we want to see." Mahatma Gandhi
3. "The time is always right to do the right thing." Martin Luther King Jr.
4. "The peacemakers shall be called the children of God." Matthew 5:9
5. "An eye for an eye leaves everybody blind." Martin Luther King Jr.

I acknowledge my child has successfully completed chapter 8.

_____   _____
Parent/Guardian's Signature   Date

CHAPTER 9
SMART SAVER

Letter to Parent/Guardian

Dear Parent/Guardian,

We are starting chapter 9 on _____ (Date). In this chapter, we will learn the importance of saving. Additionally, by the end of this section, your child will learn about being involved in an organization and giving of his/her time and talent to assist other individuals.

The following guest speakers will be invited to address the students:

1. Someone from a civic organization to speak on, *"Helping the less fortunate in your Community."*
2. A representative from a bank or credit union who will give students tips on saving for the future and managing a savings account.

Warmest regards,

_____
Guidance Counselor/Teacher

BONDING ACTIVITY
Assist your child in developing good saving habits by each of you saving a dollar a day.

Phil. 2: 4 – "Look not only to your needs but also to the needs of others."

It is vital for you to become money conscious at an early age, this includes saving, spending, donating and investing. Commonwealth Bank has a *Kids Savings Club and a Christmas Account.* Bank of The Bahamas encourages young people to open *a Junior Account* with as little as $20. First Caribbean International Bank offers the *Sure Start* to children. Fidelity Bank invites people to start A*sue* accounts with them. Credit Unions are another option for saving. If you learn how to save, you will also learn about sacrificing, doing without to get some of the things you want. You will appreciate the Xbox, tablet or PS3 game purchased with monies you saved.

According to the January – June 2016 edition of *"The Bahamas Investor,"* "There is a terribly low household savings rate in The Bahamas." Students must learn how to be frugal.

If you don't already have a savings account, ask you mummy, daddy, older brother or older sister to assist you with opening a bank account. Then when you have accumulated some money in your piggy bank, ask someone to take you to the bank so you can deposit your money into your savings account.

Instructions: Students will practice filling out deposit slips and balancing saving accounts.

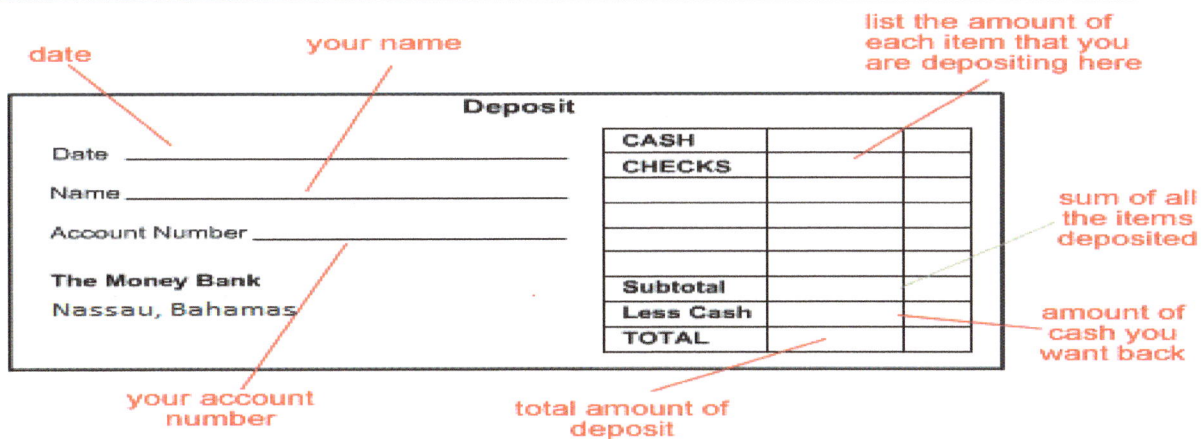

YOU CAN SAVE MORE

$1.00 a day for 365 days = a WHOPPING $365.00 for one year.

20__	January	February	March	April	May	June	July	August	September	October	November	December
1												
2												
3												
4												
5												
6												
7												
8												
9												
10												
11												
12												
13												
14												
15												
16												
17												
18												
19												
20												
21												
22												
23												
24												
25												
26												
27												
28												
29												
30												
31												
Total												

"It is more blessed to give than receive." Acts 20:35. Not only should you be concerned about saving, but you should also use your time, talent and treasure for the benefit of others. It is alright to:

- ❖ Give to others.
- ❖ Donate to charity.
- ❖ Share your lunch with your classmate who doesn't have lunch.
- ❖ Give the less fortunate boy the pair of tennis shoes that have gotten too small for you.

TIME TALENT TREASURE

How do you use your time, talent and treasure? You can use them to:

- ✓ Volunteer and help the less fortunate
- ✓ Become a Defense Force Ranger, Join Urban Renewal, Junior Achievement or Youth Empowerment Program.

Get involved. Children who are members of clubs and organizations perform better in school than children who are idle and are not members of clubs or organizations. As a member of a club or organization, you give of your time by attending the meetings and events planned by the club. You give of your talent by helping to sell goods or decorating or even writing something for the club. You give of your treasure by donating your money to the club when paying dues or helping with a fundraising event.

Instruction: Students will research local civic organizations. They will then make key holders, sell them and donate the funds to an organization. Students will generate a list of places where they can perform volunteer work.

Crawfish traps, South Andros, Bahamas
"Use your time wisely."

I acknowledge my child has successfully completed chapter 9.

_____   _____

Parent/Guardian's Signature   Date

CHAPTER 10
PARENTAL INVOLVEMENT

Letter to Parent/Guardian

Dear Parent/Guardian,

We are starting chapter 10 on _____ (Date). This chapter seeks to encourage you to become fully involved in the success of your child. Additionally, this section will focus on how you should monitor your child's use of the internet and how you can foster a better relationship with your child.

Warmest regards,

_____
Guidance Counselor/Teacher

BONDING ACTIVITY
Together with your child, create a list of activities you can do to foster a better relationship.

_____
_____
_____
_____
_____
_____
_____

Proverbs 29:15 "The rod and reproof give wisdom, but a child left to himself brings shame to his/her parents."

PARENTAL SUPPORT

Your child needs your help transitioning into Junior High School. He/she has been in the same Primary School with the same friends for at least six years. This transitional period could be a most difficult time, but with your help, parents, it could happen quickly and without incident.

TIPS FOR PARENTS

1. Spend quality time with your child – take your child to the mall, the movies, the beach.
2. Know the administrators, guidance counselor, and teachers – get email addresses and phone contacts.
3. Get to know your child's friends – get the name of parents and phone contacts.
4. Check your child's books – go over classwork and homework.
5. Attend and participate in Parents Teachers Association (P.T.A.) Meetings.
6. Make it easy for your child to communicate with you. Encourage him/her to talk to you about what is happening in his/her life.
7. Encourage your child to be respectful to administrators, teachers and fellow students.
8. Encourage your child to follow the rules of the school and society.
9. Get help for your child if necessary. If your child is struggling in a subject, get a tutor.
10. Spend quality time with your child – go for lunch together, cook/bake together.

Very seldom you get a second opportunity to do the right thing with the same child. I encourage you to be the best parent you can be. By doing this, you will have a better home, we will have a better society and all of us will make The Bahamas the best little country on the face of God's earth.

MONITOR YOUR CHILD'S USE OF THE INTERNET

The internet is vital in today's society. Businesses can have their physical building in one country while operating their back office in another country. However, parents need to teach their children how to use the internet responsibly. Tell your child you will be monitoring his/her use of the web often. Let your child know there will be no privacy when it comes to the internet. You will need to know who he/she is communicating with on the web. He/she must give you every password he/she uses, or you will create one for him/her for all his/her internet accounts. Your child will have absolutely no privacy on the web.

The following should help you to keep some degree of knowledge about your child's internet use.

1. Password protect your home computer, so you can monitor the amount of time your child spends on the web – Do not use passwords like:

a. Your date of birth   b. Your mother's name   c. Your middle name

2. When creating a password try to mix letters with numbers and symbols; this makes it very challenging for your child to figure out your password.

3. Check your computer's internet history regularly to see which sites your child has been visiting and if they're instant messaging.
4. Let them know you're monitoring their email and messaging accounts to see who they're talking to online.
5. After initial arguments with your child, he/she will understand, and it should help to prevent accusations of snooping later on.

Talk to your child about the possible dangers of chatting with strangers online and protecting private information (name, phone number, even what school they go to) and never sharing their password information with friends.

Parents, always keep the computer in the family room so you can monitor your child's use of the computer. Limit the amount of time spent on the computer. **Assign screen time for your child.** Never allow your child to have a computer in his/her room.

Children use many terms when texting. Parents, here are some terms that your child may use when texting:

1. POS – parent over shoulder
2. BOL – be on later
3. WAY – where you at
4. ETC – everything cool
5. LMIRL – let's meet in real life
6. PAL – parents are listening
7. LMBO – laughing my butt off
8. HMU – hit me up
9. CD9 – code 9, parents around
10. "Slay" – doing something very well
11. 53X – sneaky way to type sex
12. KML – killing myself laughing
13. SMT – suck my teeth
14. IWSN – I want sex now
15. FWB – friends with benefit
16. IKR – I know right
17. OMG – Oh my God
18. LOL – laugh out loud
19. " Lit" – something awesome
20. "Trapsy" - troublesome

HANDS-ON PARENTAL INVOLVEMENT
1. Show your child love – give him hugs and kisses regularly.
2. Speak positively into his/her spirit.
3. Encourage your child to have an "I can do it" attitude.
4. Assure him/her you are his/her number one fan and will always be there for him/her.

Glass Window Bridge, Eleuthera, Bahamas

PARENT'S PLEDGE

1. I will **HELP** my child to graduate as an Honor Roll student.
2. I will **TEACH** my child to be respectful to administrators, staff and fellow students.
3. I will **INSTRUCT** my child to obey the school's rules.
4. I will **ENSURE** my child attends school properly dressed each day.
5. I will **GUARANTEE** my child has all the necessary materials for each class every day.
6. I will **ENSURE** my child comes to school in good health each day.
7. I will **ENCOURAGE** my child to have a positive attitude.
8. I will **REINFORCE** an "I can" attitude in my child.
9. I will **TEACH** my child how to say, "*please,*" "*thank you,*" "*pardon me,*" "*excuse me,*" "*may I,*" "*yes sir,*" "*no sir,*" "*yes ma'am,*" "*no ma'am,*" etc.
10. I will **PRAISE** my child when he/she does well, and when challenged, **ENCOURAGE** him/her.

WHAT I LEARNED …

Congratulations! I commend you for completing *Transitioning into Junior High School.* You are now equipped with skills that will help you develop into a well-rounded individual. You will succeed. You will be an 'A' student at your new school. Use the space below to write one thought that you will remember about each chapter of the book, and how it can help you develop into the successful person you are capable of becoming.

Chapter 1……The Journey Begins _____
_____

Chapter 2 ….. Results Oriented _____
_____

Chapter 3……Your Guidance Counselor _____
_____

Chapter 4……Study Skills _____
_____

Chapter 5……I am Special _____
_____

Chapter 6 ….. Proper Use of the Internet & Electronic Devices_____
_____

Chapter 7……Anger Management _____
_____

Chapter 8……Conflict Resolution _____
_____

Chapter 9……Smart Saver _____
_____

Chapter 10…..Parental Involvement _____
_____

Minnis / Junior High School / 64

APPENDIX A
STUDENT PROGRESS REPORT

SCHOOL: _____ **DATE:** _____

STUDENT: _____ **GRADE:** _____

Your child is a capable student who has lots of ability. To ensure your child realizes his/her full potential, have your child's teachers complete this form, and return it to you so you can monitor his/her progress in school. Have this Student Progress Report form completed once monthly.

SUBJECTS	GRADES TO DATE	TEACHER	COMMENTS	TEACHER'S SIGNATURE
English Language				
English Literature				
Mathematics				
Biology				
Physical Education				
Family Life				
Religion				
History				
Geography				
_____				
_____				
_____				
_____				

	PLEASE SELECT THE APPROPRIATE COMMENT(S):			
1	Student worked well		9	Excessive talking
2	Student was punctual		10	Student was disruptive
3	Student behaved well		11	Student is tardy
4	Behavior is improving		12	Disrespectful
5	Has all school supplies		13	Refuses to cooperate
6	Completes assignments		14	Needs continual guidance
7	Cooperative, helpful, respectful		15	Parent Conference needed
8	Student has made tremendous improvement			

APPENDIX B
EMERGENCY CONTACT NUMBERS

CALL ANY ONE OF THE FOLLOWING AGENCIES FOR HELP:

AGENCIES	*PHONE*	*PHONE*	*PHONE*
ADOLESCENT HEALTH SERVICES	328-3248/9		
AIDS SECRETARIAT	328-2260	323-5968	325-2281
ALCOHOLIC ANONYMOUS	322-1685		
BAHAMAS NATIONAL DRUG COUNCIL	325-4633/4	326-5355	326-5340
CHILD ABUSE HOTLINE (GRAND BAHAMA)	351-7763		
CHILD ABUSE HOTLINE (NEW PROVIDENCE)	322-2763	422-2763	
CHILD PROTECTION SERVICES	397-2550		
CHRISTIAN COUNSELING CENTER	323-7000		
COMMUNITY COUNSELING & ASSESSMENT CENTER	323-3293		
COMMUNITY MENTAL HEALTH	323-3295/9		
CRIMINAL INVESTIGATION UNIT	322-2561	322-2562	
CRISIS CENTER (GRAND BAHAMA)	352-4357		
CRISIS CENTER (NEW PROVIDENCE)	328-0922	322-4999	
DEPARTMENT OF SOCIAL SERVICES	397-2524		
DOMESTIC VIOLENCE	323-0171	323-3859	
DRUG ENFORCEMENT UNIT	323-7139	323-7140	
HEALTH SOCIAL SERVICES – FAMILY VIOLENCE	356-3350	356-4468	
NATIONAL HOTLINE	322-2763	422-2763	
NATIONAL LEAD INSTITUTE	328-5323	525-3749	698-6384
NORTHEASTERN ALLIANCE SUSPENSION PROGRAM	356-3103/5	356-2158	
PACE SCHOOL	356-0943		
POLICE	911	919	
POLICE VICTIM SUPPORT	328-5670		
PUBLIC HEALTH DEPARTMENT	502-4700	322-8835	
SANDILANDS REHABILITATION CENTER	364-9600		
SCHOOL PSYCHOLOGICAL SERVICES	502-2948		
SURE	341-2949		
SUSPECTED CHILD ABUSE AND NEGLECT UNIT (SCAN)	322-5823	323-8438	
T.A.P.S.	393-0706	393-0672	394-3064

APPENDIX C

School Supplies

- Pencil pouch
- Blue or black pens
- No. 2 pencils
- Pencil sharpener
- Highlighters
- Permanent markers
- Erasers
- Three-ring binders
- Three-hole punch
- Loose-leaf paper
- Black & White notebooks
- Graph paper
- Folders
- Glue
- Post-its
- Wite-Out
- Protractor
- Ruler
- Scissors
- Calculator
- Book bag
- P.E. Kit
- Hand sanitizers
- Textbooks required by the school

APPENDIX D
STUDENT INFORMATION SHEET

The job of your Guidance Counselor is to assist you. Please complete this form and return it to your counselor at the beginning of the term.

NAME OF STUDENT: _____

DATE OF BIRTH: _____

PRIMARY SCHOOL: _____

HOMEROOM CLASS: _____ HOMEROOM TEACHER: _____

MOTHER'S NAME: _____

PHONE (H)_____ (C)_____ (W) _____

FATHER'S NAME: _____

PHONE (H)_____ (C)_____ (W) _____

STUDENT LIVES WITH: _____

PHONE (H)_____ (C)_____ (W) _____

Do you have any medical/emotional problems that have been medically diagnosed and may affect you during the course of the day? E.g., Asthmatic, depression, heart condition: ☐ YES   ☐ NO

If yes, please list medical/emotional problems: _____

Medication(s) being used: _____

Do you have any known allergies?   ☐ YES   ☐ NO

If yes, please list allergies: _____

Medication(s) being used: _____

GRADE 3	GLAT RESULTS
ENGLISH LANGUAGE	
MATHEMATICS	
GRADE 6	**GLAT RESULTS**
ENGLISH LANGUAGE	
MATHEMATICS	
SCIENCE	
SOCIAL STUDIES	

YOUR INTEREST/TALENT

Please place a tick next to the item(s) you are good at:

Artist: ☐ painting ☐ drawing ☐ craft

Agriculture: ☐ growing things (fruits & vegetables and/or flowers)

Athlete: ☐ track and field ☐ basketball ☐ soccer ☐ swimming ☐ volleyball Other _____

☐ Building things from wood ☐ drawing a house plan

☐ Cooking ☐ baking

Computer: ☐ creating videos ☐ repairing the computer ☐ graphics Other _____

Electronics: ☐ repairing clocks, television, computers, etc.

☐ Fixing hair ☐ barbering

Music: ☐ play an instrument ☐ sing ☐ write music ☐ dance Other _____

Writing: ☐ songs ☐ poetry

APPENDIX E

Parent/Guardian Consent Form
for Group Counseling

I give permission for my child, _____ of grade _____
to participate in Group Counseling activities.

The Group Counseling will run from _____ to _____ .

Some of the subjects to be covered in the group are as follows:
_____
_____

This group will be led by (Ms., Mrs., Mr.) _____ of
the Guidance Department.

The group leader(s) will keep the information shared by group members confidential, except in situations where:

1. Any student reveals information about harm to himself/herself or any other person.
2. Any child discloses information about abuse or molestation.
3. Any child divulges information about criminal activity, or the court (a judge) subpoenas counseling records.

The counselor is mandated to report the information immediately to the relevant authority.

By signing this form, I give my informed consent for my child to participate in Group Counseling.

Please print parent/guardian's name _____

Signature of parent/guardian _____

Please print student's name _____

Signature of student _____

Date _____

APPENDIX F

Parent/Guardian Consent Form
for Individual Counseling

I give permission for the Guidance Counselor, (Ms., Mrs., Mr.) _____
to conduct Individual Counseling with my child, _____ of
grade _____.

The Individual Counseling sessions will run from _____ to
_____.

The relationship between counselor and client relies on trust. The counselor will keep the information shared by the student confidential, except in situations where:

1. The student reveals information about harm to himself/herself or any other person.
2. The child discloses information about abuse or molestation.
3. The child divulges information about criminal activity, or the court (a judge) subpoenas counseling records.

The information must be reported to the relevant authority immediately.

By signing this form, I give my informed consent for my child to participate in Individual Counseling.

Please print parent/guardian's name _____
Signature of parent/guardian _____
Please print student's name _____
Signature of student _____
Date _____

APPENDIX G
CERTIFICATE OF COMPLETION

School _____

CERTIFICATE OF COMPLETION

This certificate is awarded to

_____

Congratulations! You have successfully completed *Transitioning Into Junior High School*.

_____
Guidance Counselor/Teacher

_____
Parent/Guardian

Date: _____

REFERENCES

Bahamas Secondary School Drug Prevalence Survey 2012 by National Anti-Drug Secretariat, The Bahamas National Drug Council

The Parent Institute

Courtesy of "How to Get Good Grades by Lee County Public Schools

Positive Classroom Management by Terri Breeden & Emaliee Egan

Annunciation BVM Catholic Elementary

Cyberbullying & Sexting: What Parents Need to Know.

The Champion's Ride by Allison Manswell

Skills for Living by Rosemarie Smead

Photos: www.bahamasweekly.com

The Bahamas Investor January – June 2016 edition

MEET THE AUTHOR

Carol D. Minnis worked as a classroom teacher for fifteen (15) years and as a Guidance Counselor for fourteen (14) years. She started her teaching career at Hawksbill High School in Grand Bahama, then moved to Central Andros High School, her alma mater. She later served at L.W. Young Junior/Senior High School, Doris Johnson Senior High School, C.V. Bethel Senior High School, C.I. Gibson Senior High School and is currently posted at the Transitional Alternative Program for Students (T.A.P.S.). Ms. Minnis has interacted with students from all strata of society.

Ms. Minnis completed her graduate studies at Kent State University in collaboration with the now, University of The Bahamas, obtaining a Master of Education in School Counseling. Her Bachelor of Science degree is in Secondary Education from Fort Valley State University, Fort Valley, Georgia. She obtained her high school education at Central Andros High School, Andros, Bahamas.

Ms. Minnis is presently serving as a Guidance Counselor and is employed by the Ministry of Education. As department head and grade level counselor, she worked tirelessly implementing programs to help students realize their full potential. She enjoys working with teenagers and gets much joy out of helping them become responsible and productive citizens.

She is a member of Holy Cross Anglican Church where she serves as an usher. Her favorite scripture verses are Romans 8:28, *"For all things work together for good to those who love The Lord, for those who are called according to His purpose."* Ephesians 3:20 *"Now unto Him, that can do **exceedingly**, abundantly above all that we ask or think, or **imagine**."*

Her hobbies include traveling, reading and gardening.

"Leaving Primary School is the next step to the future."
Rudolph Brutus, Grade 6, Claridge Primary School

Change, in general, is hard for most people, but it is an inevitable part of life. As a school counselor, I found the most difficult transition period for most students is that of Primary School into Junior High School. Carol Minnis, my colleague and friend, has created a genius piece of work, which bridges the gap between graduating primary school and entering the unknown of junior high. ***Transitioning into Junior High School*** is an interactive, fun, creative piece that takes the guesswork out of what to expect and handling the culture of the Junior High School. This "must have" book is not only an asset to school counseling but a useful tool that will aid teachers and parents as they help new students embrace change and advance successfully.

– Tamika N. Rolle, M. S.
School Counselor, Junior School Division
L. N. Coakley High School
Moss Town Exuma, The Bahamas

I am deeply appreciative of this valuable tool which is not only perfect for me as a parent but also as a Guidance Counselor. Carol Minnis' book, ***Transitioning into Junior High School*** will definitely make the transition to Junior High School an easier one while at the same time allowing parents to be actively involved in this process with their child. The exercises in this book will prepare students for the journey through high school and should be a part of every school's library.

Mrs. Andra Brown, Guidance Coordinator
C.I. Gibson Senior High School

After reading, ***Transitioning into Junior High School,*** I believe this book was written for the masses; a book that was well composed to TRANSFORM, CULTIVATE, MOTIVATE, and GUIDE the next generation and beyond.

Ms. Richine Bethel, Guidance Counselor
Mt. Carmel Preparatory Academy

With the downturn in the economy, our son will be attending public school, grade 7, for the first time at age 11. We are confident ***Transitioning into Junior High School*** will help him settle quickly and adjust to public school life. We are convinced with him using this book he will continue to excel as an Honor Roll student.

Mr. Fabian and Mrs. Joy Cartwright, Parents

Transitioning into Junior High School is a Bahamian book that will be beneficial to every child in junior high schools in the Commonwealth of The Bahamas. It depicts pictures from throughout The Bahamas:
1. *Mount Alvernia*, Cat Island
2. *Fort Montague*, Nassau, N.P.
3. *First Baptist Church*, Andros
4. *Eco Summer Camp,* Andros
5. *Crawfish Traps,* Andros
6. *Glass Window Bridge,* Eleuthera

This interactive resource book will undoubtedly alleviate the fears of both parent and child as the child begins junior school. Also, it will assist the counselor in making delivery of the counseling sessions lively and provocative.

www.ingramcontent.com/pod-product-compliance
Lightning Source LLC
Chambersburg PA
CBHW042014150426
43196CB00002B/35